SOMEONE HURT ME

SOMEONE HURT ME

Susan Cavaciuti

ENHANCEMENT BOOKS

Bloomingdale, Illinois

SOMEONE HURT ME

Susan Cavaciuti

Printed by Imago Productions in Singapore, Malaysia

Published by:

ENHANCEMENT BOOKS
P.O. Box 544
Bloomingdale, IL 60108
USA
(630) 876-0426
www.vitalhealth.net
vitalhealth@compuserve.com

ISBN: 1-890995-20-7

This book is dedicated to my friend and mentor, Dr. John Diamond, M.D. It would not have been possible to write this book without his support, and I will always be grateful to him for his wisdom and knowledge, his patience and inspiration. Thank you.

Someone hurt me.

I don't know what to do!

Something is lost

— I'm not the same as I used to be.

I feel sad

– where do I go?

I feel bad

– am I to blame?

I feel trapped

— nowhere to run.

I feel angry

— why did it happen to me?

I feel alone

— no one to talk to.

I feel scared

– who can I trust?

I'm so confused

— everything is a jumble!

"Then listen to me,"
said a voice inside.

"There are friends you can trust!"

"There are people who will listen."

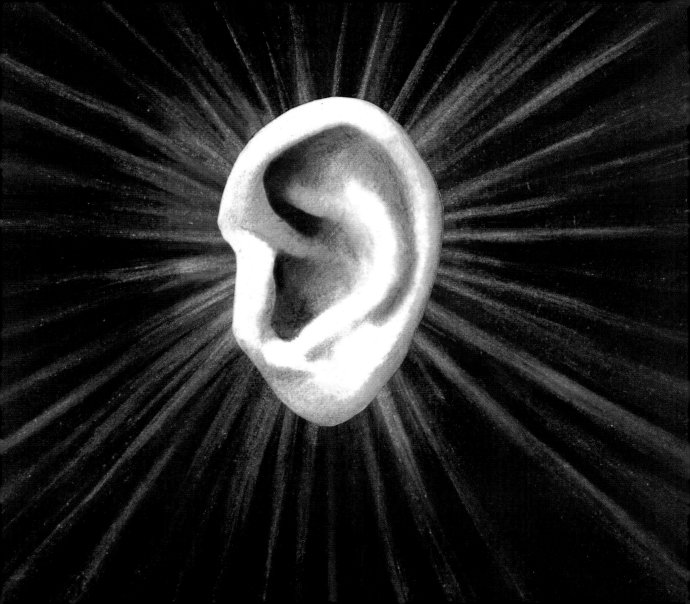

The shadow is gone.

Your spirit is with you.

Nothing is lost.

You are not alone –

"I am with you."

How to Use This Book

Someone Hurt Me is designed as a communication link to an abused child. It offers a way to reach inside the child, helping them to express their troubled emotions. The illustrations guide the child through the darkness and pain (black and white pictures with a shadowy figure), through their questions and jumbled emotions (abstract dark and bright images), and into the light (colorful scenery and bright sun). The butterfly is a symbol of change through struggle, freedom from restraint, and beauty radiating from within.

For the person supporting the child and helping them to come to terms with their emotions, it is suggested that the book be read as follows:

1) Sit together in a quiet, medium-lit room on comfortable chairs or sofa.
2) Offer food and drink, as needed.
3) Tissues should be readily available.
4) The child may hold a comfort toy, if they like.
5) A familiar adult may sit nearby, if appropriate.

The following suggestions may also assist the support person in reaching out to the traumatized child:

1) Maintain constant contact with the child and have someone else record the session, if necessary.

2) Read the book slowly, taking time to view the illustrations and answer questions as truthfully as possible.
3) Use your intuition to guide you through the book.
4) If the child is upset, give them time to recover.
5) It is important that the child be led through the book, as if they are on a journey.
6) Don't get stuck in the middle of the book as emotions come to the surface. Take whatever time is needed to finish the book.
7) Emphasis should be placed on the fact that the child's sense of power has not been taken away, but that it is still with them.
8) Offer comfort to the child and let them know they are not to blame.
9) Remember to get support for yourself, to clear yourself of any negative feelings that have arisen in you so that you can support the next child.

Children's Support Services

Child at Risk Hotline
1-800-792-5200

Child Help USA,
National Child Abuse Hotline
1-800-4-A-CHILD
1-800-2-A-CHILD (T.D.D.)

Child Lures, Ltd.
5166 Shelburne Road
Shelburne, VT 05482
Tel: (802) 985-8458
Fax: (802) 985-8418
www.childlures.org

Justice for Children
1-800 733-0059

Children's Institute International
711 S. New Hampshire Ave.
Los Angeles, CA 90005
Tel: (213) 385-5100
Fax (213) 383-1820
www.childrensinstitute.org

National Runaway Switchboard
1-800-621-4000

Prevent Child Abuse America
200 S. Michigan Avenue, 17th Floor
Chicago, IL 60604-2404
Tel: (312) 663-3520
Fax: (312) 939-8962
www.preventchildabuse.org

Professional Support Services

American Professional Society on
the Abuse of Children (APSAC)
National Office
407 S. Dearborn Street, Suite 1300
Chicago, IL 60605
Tel: (312) 554-0166
Fax: (312) 554-0919
www.apsac.org

The International Society for the
Prevention of Child Abuse and
Neglect (ISPCAN)
200 North Michigan Avenue
Suite 500
Chicago, IL 60601
Tel: (312) 578-1401
Fax: (312) 578-1405
www.ispcan.org

National CASA Association
100 W. Harrison St. North Tower
Suite 500
Seattle, WA 98119
Tel: (800) 628-3233
Fax: (206) 270-0078
www.nationalcasa.org

Sidran Traumatic Stress Foundation
200 E. Joppa Road, Suite 207
Towson, MD 21286
Tel: (410) 825-8888
www.sidran.org

About the Author

Susan Cavaciuti graduated from the College of Art and Design in Portsmouth, England in 1987. A Celtic artist, Susan captures light and movement in her work, striving to create three-dimensional images in a variety of media: pastels, oils, watercolor, mixed media, needlework, ceramics, sculpture and photography. Her work has been purchased for display in private collections, and she has given exhibitions in France, England, and the United States.

Susan is also an illustrator whose publication credits include: **My Whole Foods ABC's** (a picture book for children), **Stevia Sweet Recipes: Sugar - Free Naturally!** and **Taste Life! The Organic Choice**. Her first individually authored book, **Someone Hurt Me**, is a picture book for children with a history of trauma and abuse.

Mrs. Cavaciuti explains her reasons for writing this book:

As a trauma and abuse survivor, I know that one of the most harmful outcomes of abusive situations is the victim's inability to express their feelings: the pain, humiliation, helplessness, sadness, confusion and anger. In my case, I found my sense of power and strength taken away from me, leaving me as a paralyzed child, with all my emotions bottled up inside, ready to explode. Unable to verbalize these feelings, I found an outlet through Art. The very act of creating helped me to release my emotions and conflicts, putting me on the road to recovery and healing.

I have therefor dedicated my life to breaking the cycle of abuse, using the Creative Arts as a healing modality. I hope to enhance the quality of life for abuse sufferers and activate their will to be well, teaching them to creatively express their deepest and highest selves. And through exhibitions and publications, I hope to increase community awareness, understanding and acceptance of people with a history of trauma and abuse.

Therapeutically, Susan is a Consultant in Arts for Health and a graduate of the Institute for Music and Life Enhancement. She works to help others by encouraging and nurturing their creativity and has extensive professional and clinical experience with children and adults with a variety of problems: mental health disorders, physical disabilities, and autism.

Regarding the role of art in therapy, Mrs. Cavaciuti explains:

I believe that the primary purpose of Art is to heal. That the artist expresses not only their feelings and emotions, but their journey through their suffering - from the pit of despair to the realization that they are loved, so that the viewer is uplifted and inspired to positively view and express their own journey, which in turn will inspire others.

Susan currently serves as a consultant in Creative Arts For Health at the Community Support Day Program in Holyoke, MA. The program provides therapeutic, creative and vocational programs for adults with mental health and substance abuse problems.

Susan Cavaciuti

Also from Vital Health Publishing/Enhancement Books:

My Whole Food ABC's

David Richard and Susan Cavaciuti

My Whole Food ABC's serves as a primer for teaching children the value of healthy, natural foods. Simple rhymes and colorful illustrations associate whole foods with the letters of alphabet, encouraging young ones to learn both the ABC's and the basics of sound nutrition.

ISBN: 1-890612-07-3, 28 pp., 6-1/2" x 7" paperback.

$8.95